Barefoot

A COLLECTION OF POEMS

ANN ROUSSEAU

ISBN: 0615479251
ISBN-13: 9780615479255
Library of Congress Control Number: 2011928183

Author photo: Charles Salomons

The single, smooth stone
is lost to the pattern.

Oh, my imperfect eye,
what more have you missed?

Compo Beach,
Westport, 1975

Contents

OUT THERE

LATER

Acknowledgements

Many of us who write poetry do so because we need to write poetry; perhaps we are searching for clarity in our experiences.

There are challenges with the form. A word or phrase twists and turns in the night, keeping us from rest. We confront the limitations of language. These issues can only be balanced by the incredible joy, the delight, in completing a poem that pleases. Sharing those poems also brings great pleasure.

To those who have appreciated my work, I am especially grateful. I give thanks to Jackie Kelly, Ed Gomez, and Bill Lowney for letting me know that one of my poems has somehow touched them.

 I give thanks to Penny Liu and Bill McCarthy for their support and guidance during the years of our writing group; and I give special thanks to my biggest fans, my husband Jeffrey and my daughter Daryl.

Ann Rousseau
April 2011

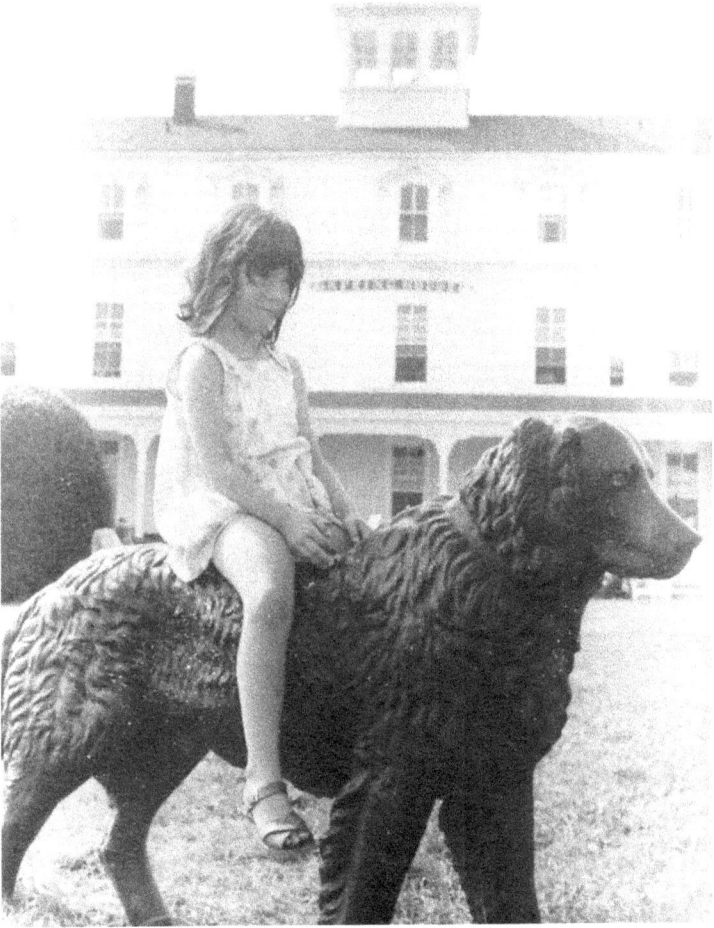

Early

Gaia

If
at first tremor, granite which
cold under foot and hard
were to shatter paper-thin and free
(the solid crust which holds us all
crumbling in dust-soft kisses to rest),

Who would contain the fire,
shore up the walls against storm,
lift to heaven dream-castle spires?

Who would rock the cradle
That holds the sleeping child?

Ann Rousseau

In a Garden

In a garden
distant giants grumble;
white blossoms en pointe,
stretch to gather approaching gifts.

Clear water falls from dark clouds,
splashes on green tongues
stretched skyward,
washes stones smooth.

The garden celebrates life,
this day,
this moment.

Words, phrases, and images
circle in groups,
collect in puddles.

I listen and watch.
I study the stones.

River Grasses

Tall river grasses
sway above warm water;
greens heavy with moisture
fall to mirror's edge.

A boat
enameled in gloss,
layers red and rich,
plumbs muddy waters,
searching with the heart
through things familiar.

Winter Delight

Treetops
glazed in sunlight
glisten in morning,
a thousand glass stems
tinkling in unison.

Snow
soft as angel wings
hovers in evening,
a blanket of quiet
settling in soft mounds.

Enough of beauty!
My back aches from shoveling.
I shiver against the wind.
I was not born for such a world
where steps must be measured.

Yet on days
when Heaven's warmth again surrounds
and the green of treetops whispers,
I will walk in sunlight unfettered,
recalling the joy of winter.

Green Morning

The carpenter's hammer,
drumming still the bird-talk,
raps industriously on the morning.

Weeds,
taller than I and peppered with blossom,
invite the gardener's blade.

A cat,
passing softly on wood mosses,
dreams the crunch
of bird bones.

On this day
green with purpose,
I lie dormant,
waiting for my human spring.

Orchard

Beyond innumerable seasons
lives a woman,
a mother/child who won't settle for the moment
but won't disregard it.
Burdened by history
yet wiser for it,
she must look beyond the lesson of her experiences.

She must learn to regard the dappled windfalls of the orchard,
no longer blushing and seamless,
diverse and grand in their design.

She must savor these apple-heavy mornings,
the thump of russet orbs
that resonate beyond season.

She must revisit this orchard
when brittle stems scrape a pewter sky,
light flooding the spaces between
the dark lines of incident.

She must learn to accept endings,
to trust new beginnings,
to change the habits of her heart.

Evening Walk

Long shadow fingers
mottle my path,
cool my toes.

Darkness and light
together,
patterns of experience,
woven in shifting colors,
make beautiful
my evening walk.

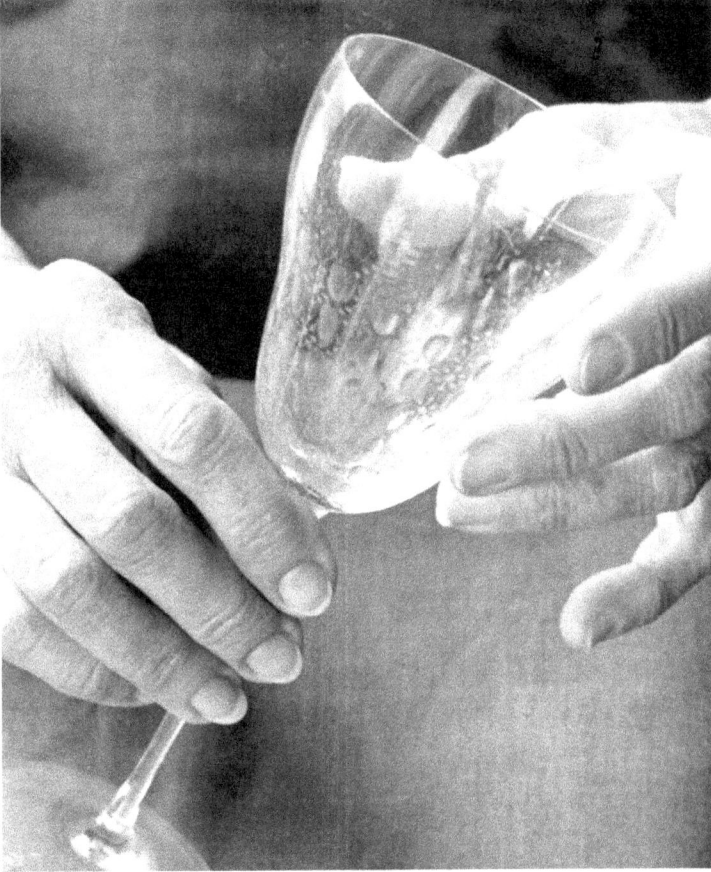

Along The Way

Barefoot

Amber toes with bleached nail crescents
dangle into cool water,
dipping into memories of burning summer sands
and rain-softened grasses
like clear lake bottoms.

Crisp mornings will follow.
One cannot remain barefoot.

Unlike blankets which can be cast off,
work shoes harness in earnest:
straps chafe,
laces pinch,
heels throw us forward into the day.

Contained and restrained,
we walk a straight path,
run a good race
no longer naked beneath summer cottons.

Only in summer
we dance.

Grackles

A form organic,
this cloud of grackles
balloons wide,
undulates,
folds in upon itself,
falling upon a field
recently gone brown.

A sudden current,
the whisper of traffic,
presses gently,
unsettles,
scatters the flock,
lifting a hundred pounding hearts
in frenzied dance.

A flurry of feathers,
this winter squall
rises wide-eyed,
rushes,
storms wild with change
while I,
with far less grace,
turn to leave.

Shells

Shells gathered yesterday
secret spirals
seaglass dreams
clutter my desk.

Salt smooth
washed from afar
captive memories
promise to stay.

Lobster

It won't be long until
the naked lobster
scurrying among jagged rocks,
his tender pink
ribboned with care,
will once again
hide scars of experience
beneath shiny red armor.

Moon Street

On this heavy day
while unsettled gray
hosts no sail,
surf ungentle
crests along damp sand,
spumes above gray stone
a soft melody once.

White gulls stand,
their backs to worldly traffic,
facing the sea, watching
as though
that which is constant
would rise up uncivil.

I live on moon street,
waiting impatiently
for tiresome tides
to rage high,
sweep this familiar beach,
spill all secrets,
change the landscape.

You Say

As you turn to leave,
you stumble.

Leaving,
you say,
is hard.

Moments like this,
you say,
hurt.

Turning to leave,
I say,
is what you do best.

And the long-sleeping child
who would not die,
awakens within me
to weep.

Unwholesome

Unwhole
some would say
to disregard such signals.
Eyes flutter and do not pause.
Fingers extend and do not touch.
Lips move and do not speak.

Unwhole
some would say
to dismiss such trappings.
Is a man not more than a season of his soul,
a heart more than the sorrow of a moment?

Some would say
you cannot embrace the clouds
or tickle the skin of the moon.
A man selects his own colors
and crafts his own ambitions.

Better to hold
some
one who walks with heavy feet,
holds rainbows in his eyes
and your breath in his arms,
a man who laughs in his sleep.

Stones

I have always been a saver of stones,
sifting though soil, selecting
chunks to fill childpockets,
carefully gathered carelessly lost
treasures.

Two stones adorn my desk:

One, a composite,
dappled and rough,
colorful and diverse,
a lover's stone
stolen from a wall,
marking a moment,
revered over time,
an anchor to the past.
When I touch it now, it crumbles.

Another, granite,
significant in size,
solid and common,
a husband's stone
saved along a summer stroll,
a shared memory
weighting papers,
an anchor to the day.
When I hold it now, it shines.

Perfect Couple

We are the perfect couple.
We complement each other.

Your laughter invades my melancholy.
My delight shatters your gloom.

Through my lens
your carefully constructed cities
are cast in roseate glow,
while I, Antaeus ungrounded,
look to your dew-heavy stems,
crisp apple mornings.

We are close.
We fill each other.
I flow around the mountains of you
and into the valleys
as rain flows,
falling
filling
providing moisture
from which
weeds may grow.

In My Favorite Photograph

In my favorite photograph
my mother's hands hold carefully
a crystal glass so delicate
she can feel the ice within.
A glass which,
unlike the hands that hold it,
was lost to its own fragility.

Those hands,
strong against change,
suffered the iron that pressed crisp my blouse,
supported the measured bag of groceries up narrow
stairs,
scrubbed shiny a place for me at the top of those stairs.

Those hands,
burnished with work,
gnarled and unadorned,
labored to exorcise the ghost of the Depression.
(You cannot live on potatoes and not be changed.)

Her hands,
those working-woman's hands,
were her humiliation,
as though poverty were the fault of the poor
and dignity the price of hard work.

In my favorite photograph
my mother's hands are so like her –
strong,
enduring, and
worn with love.

The Problem with Research

The problem with research is
that you just may discover something
that invalidates what you've been teaching
(for the past twenty years!)
And hey,
you just may not be able to find
the names and addresses of all those
students who have since remarried/moved to
Seattle/relocated out of the country,
whom you taught in good faith,
faith evidently not good enough
(We all thought gerunds were important!)
like the parent who
in good faith may have been a bad parent
but hey, after all,
was doing the best she could
at the time considering
her needs and intelligence at that moment.
And hey, after all,
teachers are human, too, and
so are their students who,
after all,
may not have been paying attention anyway.

Summer Games

The squeak of styrofoam lid against dust-smudged cooler,
the faded tee shirt across chain-link fence,
players in matching stripes on fading wooden benches,
crossed spikes tangled in wild grasses,
gloves, water jars, sports bags –
summer signals.

Old barrels with rusting bottoms
host swarms of summer bees
feasting on ice-cream wrappers and droplets of sweet soda.
We assemble on aluminum benches
that stripe and grill our thighs,
squint watching/not watching,
once again hearing
cheers of hopeful mothers,
counsel of aging fathers,
play of younger sisters –
summer sounds.

Barefoot

Red dust coats base bags,
obscures baselines,
clouds the air as
he slides into third,
stirring dust-heavy memories of
summers past.

Witness

Many, too distant to touch,
were pulled with hooks from clear water today.
I watched
and saw the traveler's soaked case floating in morning light
beside the bodies of children,
and heard a man in gray explain that condolences without
apology would be sent
and perhaps money.

This is the way of our world,
where science celebrates a single life saved against odds,
a child pulled from a shaft,
but cannot protect a plane that
strayed perhaps from a designated corridor, and
descended perhaps in four minutes, and
threatened perhaps soldiers with trained eyes and hearts
who live with imperfect instruments in an imperfect world.

Barefoot

A father crouches in mourning,
his tears lost to an angry mob.
I would grieve,
though I find it hard to embrace those whose fists
were raised in hatred before this day.

Moved by an image of suffering, my hand extends
but finds a cool, glass screen, and I am left
to witness in silence,
to watch without touching,
to await news of other travelers
pulled untimely from schedules, and
other children who will not
dance for their fathers.

Savannah Waterfront

Beneath oaks tinseled with moss,
glass-eyed tourists
sway to cabaret ballads
on city-warmed cobblestone.

Garlands of light
transform windows to carnival,
fade alleys,
hide bins of rubbish.

In shadow
as quietly as cats
picking among the ruins,
human night rats.

Florida

Amid creamsicle rows of peach and lemon stucco,
succulent greens and stately palms,
sandy borders of thirsty lawns,
red and yellow hibiscus explode.

An '82 Mercury Marquis with Bayshore plates,
heat-waffled,
carries Saul in seersucker,
Alma in pastels and gold,
freshly bathed and permed,
to early bird ritual.

A blue and white RV,
rainbowed with bumper stickers,
sun-brilliant,
houses Joe, leathered from fishing,
Joan in turquoise rollers,
spent from daily miles,
to evening homeground.

Pelicans in line on the pier
ruffle feather-heavy wings, and
glass-eyed,
turn to the horizon.

Warm Enough

Applewood burns well,
crackles red and yellow
this rainy October afternoon.

Curled into himself,
footless,
neckless,
the cat sags,
the quilt slipping
between my knees.

Childhood blankets once
shaded morning light
before first fire.
I dressed for school
beneath thick quilts,
never warm enough.

Cold October rain
taps at my window.
Ragged apple leaves
blanket the chilled ground.

Now
warm enough,
my hands cup a steaming mug
as I settle in with dusty volume
in a cat-warmed lap.
The dog groans in dream.

Manwich

I want to know
the fruit-sweet scent of your hair,
the saline veil of your exertion,
the nut-rich honey of your passion.
I want to know
if I should have you
on Wheat Thins or rye.

Obscene Phone Calls: Three Poems

Poem 1

It was 1:36 a.m.
Her foot was twisted in the sheet.
She tripped over the dog.
By the time she reached the phone,
she was sure that a loved one
was maimed, dead, or both.

So she was quite relieved,
you will understand,
to learn
that the emergency
was his
and not her own.

Poem 2

(The voice asked, "Are you naked?")

To be naked is not enough.
To lie with a stranger is deception,
a fantasy played by both who,
in stillness or in frenzy,
lie alone.

Poem 3

The deep voice began,
"If you want to see your husband alive again,
don't hang up."
We were separated at the time so
naturally
I hung up.

I don't get obscene calls anymore.
Perhaps I'm too old
or it is the economy
or the no-call list,
which doesn't deter
salesmen and politicians.

Perhaps it's the internet,
a more modern way
to remain
anonymously naughty.

Out There

Languages

Who are you
who walk silently
just outside?

Do you speak as a dancer
who carves spaces,
balancing light on the arch of his spine?

Do you speak as a poet
who whispers colors,
crafting glass-eyed swans?

Do you speak as a drop of rain
that dreams silver,
glazing quiet a blossom petal?

Hearing only your silence,
I wait to hear your language.

Gate

Gravel slips underfoot.
Muscles strain.
For all your breath
rooted stone will not move;
rusted steal will not give way.

Charge against it.
It remains.

Tug at the lock.
Shake it.
Hold in your hand
what keeps you without.

Only the gatekeeper has the key,
takes slow steps,
and may not come today.

Become as water.
Slide inside.
Flow to the place where
all that matters is.

Blossom

Membrane-thin petals,
fold upon fold,
close tightly upon
the heart that holds them
as if by warming,
it could be healed.

The delicate bud
having witnessed the Fall
turns brown with bruises
and will blossom in morning
imperfect.

Empty

Sometimes
the wind whispers
empty.

The chilled current
is drawn into
the spaces among the reeds,
warmed by straw-brittle life,
contained and expelled,
losing form and warmth
before ever realizing
beauty.

For Her Own Good

For her own good
he carefully folded the page,
placing the transparent sheet
into his coat,
a treasure within reach of
his own warm hands.
Why fan false hopes?
Why risk the fire?

For her own good
he walked away,
whispering of his love,
a most generous deed,
to limit the damage,
to temper the flames.

For her own good
thin blankets drawn
in upon himself,
his pockets stuffed with
dreams long past and faded,
he offered himself to Death,
no longer her problem,
no longer her pain.

For her own good
she faced the sunrise,
kneading her hands gently
in an effort
to make them warm.

Only the Moment

She waits for the past,
She waits for the future.

Her heart unschooled
refuses the day,
mourns loss immeasurable.

Translucent bubbles
color the morning.
She fears fancy.

To remember is to lose.
To imagine is to lose.
Tell her the moment lives,
only the moment.

Cosmic Carpenter

Dropping plumb line
from slanted moon to sand castles below,
he crafted a perfect frame.

Within
he placed carefully constructed cities,
neatly folded dreams,
stars of his intentions.

A maverick knothole
swelled beneath an errant drop of dew
too soon exploded,
filling the sky.
A cosmic kaleidoscope.

He watched as beauty
shattered and fell.
Picking up a scrap of wood,
measuring with trained eye,
carefully assembling the rubble of intentions,
he caught a star by the tail
and began again.

Invitation

Where is the place in this house
which is mine?

Undusted candlesticks clutter burnished tables,
falling to carefully chosen carpets.
Things of value press walls, test seams,
demand change.
Children, in kindness or not,
milk me of mine.
Loving animals scratch at my solitude.
I am touched too much.

Go with me to a room within.
Press forward with closed eyes.
Enter without breathing
for the air is light
in a room where memories live.

A girl before a mirror pivots, sees us,
and returns to her dance.
A woman holds to light
negatives that will not fade.

In the heart of this home,
deeper within,
French windows open onto Hawthorne's gardens.
Wildflowers, unrestrained, breathe light.
Old fences, in disrepair, whisper history.

Sit awhile in my mother's chair,
reading books with golden leaves,
feasting on warm bread and honey,
drinking tea.

Moon Poem

The moon is rolling close tonight
spinning out a silver thread
and I,
silently ascending,
leave fields of autumn amber and winter
diamonds,
earthmoments,
behind.

Moon verses fall in clouds from my lips.
Moon rhythms lighten the pulse of my steps.

The moon is rolling close tonight
spinning out a silver thread
while I,
drawn by distant symphonies,
return,
making milk-soft prints on cool grasses,
lingering in evening quiet.

Later

Seamless

Again the chimes ring two and
it's *Poker After Dark* or just
dark,
the noise of conversations
past or future
interrupting sleep.

In dreams
the bicycle lies by the curb,
its pedals spinning.
The rider rises from the fall,
unsure that balance will
ever be restored.

In dreams
the horse waits in the meadow,
its coat glistening.
The rider struggles to his back,
wondering why there is no
ease in the remount.

In dreams
wrinkled images without transition
bump and knock
clatter
clutter
blend in unholy harmonies with
rhythms of the day.

Frayed chords
bind one fragment to the next,
scattered sounds
without music.

Why do we expect the night
to be seamless?
Our days are never more than
a discordant progression of experiences
without clarity
without pattern
without symmetry.

Traces

The residue of our deeds lingers,
clings to our days and our dreams,
coloring ever so slightly
our moments.

As weighty as Marley's chains,
the grit of experience settles.

Those who bumped against us in life,
each with his own story,
live now in memory,
informing our thoughts.

Past joys fuel our hopes.
Sorrows press low our spirits.
Traces remain,
becoming the lens of our perception.

Music

Before dawn,
curtains
no longer hover
but stand,
the air
heavy with rain,
sweet and thick.

Below
tires hiss along moist pavement,
solid and sure.

On a newer road,
satinsmooth and slick,
water runs in sheets.

On an older road,
crumbling and gritty,
water pools in ditches.

A third road,
worn with experience,
collects a blanket of moisture,
holds the warmth of days past,
shimmers in the last minutes of the streetlight.

This road
makes music.

Self-Doubt

I saw it but did not know it.
I recorded it but did not understand it.
I gave it a moment but wondered why
anyone really
needed to hear it.

Peach

Less than gracefully
I peel back
the skin to
this dry day.

This leathered peach,
this juiceless pith, holds
just enough moisture
for one more
poem.

Lace

Connected to this world
tentatively
by silk threads to slivered branches,
I weave
within and without
His grace,
stopping only
now and again
to touch green stems and mottled leaves.

Laboring to hold fast
one more day,
this spinner
is too near to see
lace
brilliant with morning moisture.